CONTROL
SUPPRESS
DELETE

CONTROL SUPPRESS DELETE

Angela Hibbs

Palimpsest Press
1171 Eastlawn Ave.
Windsor, Ontario. N8S 3J1
www.palimpsestpress.ca

Book and cover design by Dawn Kresan. Printed offset on Rolland Zephyr Laid at Coach House Printing in Ontario, Canada. Edited by Jim Johnstone. Cover photograph of Mary St-Amand Williamson's performance installation, "Yellow Umbrella" New York, 2015 by Chun Hua Catherine Dong.

Palimpsest Press would like to thank the Canada Council for the Arts, and the Ontario Arts Council for their support of our publishing program. We also acknowledge the assistance of the Government of Ontario through the Ontario Book Publishing Tax Credit.

Canada Council for the Arts Conseil des Arts du Canada
ONTARIO ARTS COUNCIL
CONSEIL DES ARTS DE L'ONTARIO
Ontario
Ontario Media Development Corporation

Library and Archives Canada Cataloguing in Publication

Hibbs, Angela, 1978–, author
Control suppress delete / Angela Hibbs.

Poems.
Issued in print and electronic formats.
ISBN 978-1-926794-49-5 (softcover)
ISBN 978-1-926794-50-1 (PDF)

I. TITLE.

PS8615.I33C66 2017 C811'.6 C2017-902876-6
C2017-902877-4

For Dad

JUNE 3, 1958 – MARCH 13, 2016

CONTENTS

WATERBEARER

There are few vessels more human
than the bottle. The neck, the chest.

I become a member of a club.
Will I become a member of another club?

The twist of the wrist
atop these urns

is a ritual of respect
for the number of turns
it takes to remove the twisted top.

ASHES, DOWNTOWN VANCOUVER

Diamond encrusted bodybags
make way for the breathtaking purse.

Hunt with a grenade to fondle;
to turn down the boredom.

LOCATION, LOCATION, LOCATION

What of the lunar surface?

Can I wear it
after labour day?

Avoid the zoological park
after dark

or when you are less than logical.

What suggests the pendulum
more than an elephant's trunk?

Click here if you would like the spotted
leopard cam to alarm you
when they wake.

GIVE ME

a minute. With the days like they are,
it's hard to guess what day is.
A mitt full of index fingers.

One day to sit, another to stand.
There are fewer and fewer nicks.
Not enough to stitch. No more is
the clock wise.

Line up to fill an hourglass—
The more often I look
at a clock the more it melts.

BANDAGES

There are roomettes in the library
with leather tab handles. They have
locks on them.

X remembers the civility with which Y cut him.

X crosses out remembers. Chooses recalls.

Civility is replaced with gentleness.
Gentle is not gentle enough.

If air moves it is not gentle enough.

reads the want ads becomes the nanny
in the basement looking at the wanter's wife
and two children. One Sunday, a month to
himself. More than his billion dollar ideas,
he thinks, it is his ability to put himself in
other people's shoes that makes him tall.

"I don't dream NY or Central park or lots of places (which I secretly think belong to me)" —DIANE ARBUS, LETTER 1952

A library book that none but she could appreciate.
A pair of gloves she stole to punish the price.
A necklace from a horrible cocktail party.
A bra fastened under a shirt.
A six inch screw.
One shoe, too small, pushed into her handbag.

Approaching the clerk with said shoe and asking
about the timing of new collections before
leaving with the shoe. Maybe returning it
worn would be harder still.

FREE VERSE

Seasons' causes disinterest
us. Attention drawn to drawing
quarterly. Pencils drawn and paper distant.
Drawing draws us to structure, references
bones. Weigh probability
of lead raised. Lazarus varies,
makes wishes copper-real.

Seaweed crowd deliberates.
Attend the Queen
to draw dreams.

WASPS ON A BUS

They have entered
buzzing
bussing to take
part in the sweetness.
Hair spray, pheromone spray,
bruised banana spray.
Bruised halos gather
in the shade shadow's made.
Hello, halo, hallowed sweet.

MONA LISA: OWNER'S MANUAL

Keep her in an ill lit room;
noise at a sigh.
Swaddle her in silk;
listen while she praddles—
this may take years—

of the millions who shot her,
the decades she was a souvenir,
a Renaissance pin-up girl.
Disagree when she says
her oils are sagging.

LUNGE

How useless
the umbrella
submerged.

Algae scarves
smell burnt wax
remove the arm

evenly the blanket

is fear and pain
without fear or pain

MAPPLETHORPE'S BOURGEOIS

A phallus

named "little girl"

three-foot cock cradled on the subway

MICHAEL SHANNON

You must grow your hair.
If you cannot,
hair will be provided for you.
If the hair provided for you
is nominated for an Oscar,
the identity of the hair's
grower will go untold.

BEHOLD

Fabric. Stainless steel. Glass. Wood.
Atoms. Translucence. Impermanence.
Woven. Heated. Mined. Cut.
Collect. Consume. Order.
A wine glass not broken,
plucked from its stem.

Ice sheets catapult onto a bus.
A semi drifts out of its lane.
A hill is available for vehicles
whose brakes dissolve in a glass.
Glass decomposes in one to two million years.

PORTRAIT OF ISABEL RAWSTHORNE STANDING IN A STREET IN SOHO, 1967

What splashes
out of her pocket and foot?
Will she get her hand back?
Perhaps it is daytime
her absent shadows.
She realizes she
is in a package.

RAINING COINS

It's worth a tour. Stamping makes
work for people and machines.
Work to make coins represent work.
Make work, make mint, make minions,
make millions. The cent is the only coin
stamped onto pre-made blanks.
Witness process.

EPITHALAMIUM

The house that was
on fire was ours. The jury
was out on where we'd met.
An orphan came to live with us.
We didn't mind.

Police knocked. They told us
our house was incorrectly numbered
and we hadn't been getting a lot
of our mail.
They didn't mind about the orphan

or the fire or the room shortage.
The house fire is still burning.
But it is correctly numbered.
We toss junk mail into the embers.
The magazines were antique.

We invited people over
for an old-timey party.
When nobody came, we had the inferno
to blame. It takes some getting used to.
Really, we should be grateful
for the orphan's spark.

MACHINES AT RUST

Consider crushing them,
the implications of crushing them.
The undoable.
There is nothing to do regarding the machines
but regard the machines.

MY LIFE IT STOOD A MARKET READY PRODUCT

Now that I am productive I am a product.
That is, I pee gravy.
That is, I grave chemical peels.
That is I peel out of parking lots,
Paradise Lots.

Arguments couched
in a nail bed.

What of our couches?

STRUGGLE WITHIN—AFTER LOUISE BOURGEOIS

Crawling over and crawled over
busy with my hands and mouths
and legs too, really, looking one way
seeing another, busy with his
hands, legs and mouth and every way
every one seen, every thing seen
busy at business.

AT THE LIBRARY

Leave privacy at the door

Bow to the photocopier

Staff bring aloe vera plants

Idiocy is fool proof

Vixens nuzzle me

Parse orders from the peninsula

The door mocks the floor

BLUE

Subvert the frame
Make blue blur bluer

Resist blue, spread blue, brighten blue,
make blue new, what did blue ever do
to you? You give the dew
it's due.

Berries, potatoes, too few available in blue

Cold lips, lines on paper, sky, ocean,
a child's drawing of a glass of water, one
of Picasso's periods. Purple prose
when you extract the red

Use a ruler, throw it away
Put on a skirt, let it sway

Her mission unknown
A departure postponed

Capture a pose that isn't posed
Let her appear unclothed

FRANCIS BACON'S STUDIO

HP sauce mixed
                with a palette knife
in powdered chicken soup
                tastes like filet mignon.

Sometimes the sick must sip oil
and soy sauce, to keep from slipping away.

Flashed light in his eyes
to make himself produce.

Though unclothed
his body resembles
nothing more than a pile.

THEORY OF TYPICAL BEAUTY

The inner ear discovered
in school. Thinner rears
uncovered at the pool. Organize
the notes with higher hopes. Tighten
tropes. Make it beautiful.
The beauty of the matador

just outside the door. A tool
to fool with or a million dollar
box to bang.

Play me out the door. Coat me in song.
The moon will define new.

SPIED

after Louise Bourgeois

The panels touch
they do not meet.

Have you not been
those legs?

There was no time
without mirrors.

When has a ball ever
not been
a disco ball?

More keys than locks.

A risk, a pin.

TERROR MANAGEMENT THEORY

Not having a flute
is worse than death.

There are unknown ways
to be nicer.

On the seventh day
God worked on his Pinterest.

A lemon does not expect
its juice to stay with it.

Mr. T became a Doctor
and changed his last name to Light.

The fountain of youth is full
of dinosaur spit.

Nothing attracts germs
like latex.

SPICE

The number of men who wear Old Spice,
who are currently living,
divided by those who are funny,
less those who are good at something.

A half teaspoon in the palm,
a quarter teaspoon too much.
Some bass notes can still be felt
twenty-four hours after application.

Food smells: orange, lemon, cinnamon,
vanilla. Tonka, the smells that remind you
of mom: carnation, geranium, jasmine.

Top notes are the most volatile.
He smells three hundred million dollars
in debt. American dollars!

DEMOCRACY

Ocean traffic isn't what it used to be.
In the light it shines.
By heaven, I mean painlessness.

We went north for days;
to make up for all the north,
south for weeks.
The earthers became incredible.
Then laughable.

Nobody reports back from below.
We made lists of all the animals
we never thought we'd see again.
In another column, those we'd never seen.

How people look in pajamas—
we remembered we forgot.

There's a lot to argue about.

It's not true that people retell
memorized stories to pass the time.

Commit once to suicide.

Bragging is also a way to get killed.
Most things are on the unspoken list.

A HOLE

The shovel was ill equipped to dig all
the way to hell but allowed for
clay and other riddles.

Tabled gems
no naysaying, just harvest
the ice.

Leaving without the ice: hunger.

Camaraderie is fine as well
as the singing. The mine speaks
to the minor.

Touch and
smell.

Exchange gold for cash: bijection. Sidewalked patriarchs
parse bargains, pontificate. Anon,
the wealthiest man in the poorest shoes.

The escape from
time. The view. How interested in
ocular degeneration.
Nothing but degeneration and silent too!

All that to say he put a diamond
into a woman.

(QUAINT)

She bore it. The diamond was celebrated
as diamonds are. The child
was subdermal. The child sparkled, was printed
on 100 announcements.
The child was cut with vodka.

Its poker face wasn't the half of it.

Any kindness that poker was subjected to
was dusted off. Colourblind was good enough.
Deaf, his favourite game,

Escape meant there was somewhere to be.

NOTES: TOWARDS THE BODY

Warning, the pigeons must not
be fed. In the morning, the pigeons are dead.

This information is prohibited.

The reader's nervous system
breaks promises.

Whether the sun is out or not, it is morning.

PARALYSIS

You really can't call yourself a procrastinator until you've left a dead body in the basement for a couple weeks. Turn the air conditioner up to keep the smell down. The sheet tossed over isn't much of a barrier. Dream the body disposed of. Dream killing nearer the landfill. Dream a truck crashing into the house takes blame for the death.

WHAT IS A LAKE

A small ocean   A saltless sea   A salesman asleep   A frame   A drink   A destination   A surface   River fed and stream drained   Sun burned and homeless   Temporary   Shown in the encyclopedia with a photograph   not a child's drawing

WHAT A LAKE CAN DO FOR YOU

Make your eyes more attractive
A place to pee
Talk to you about a topic of your choosing
Scare you
Please you
Be counted
Agree with everything you say
Clean your clock
Even out evil etchings
Frost your tips
Outsmart your nemesis
Knight you
Celebrate you
Remove your shortcomings
Lay you down on a bed of roses

NOW THANKS TO NEW TECHNOLOGY

skull slice
adjust frontal lobes
maximize cognition.
Instalment payments
available
lobotomist near as your

Never forget where your

! open your skull
  depress that frontal lobe.

A BRIEF HISTORY OF MASTER / SERVANT RELATIONS

Shall I compare thee to a box of crackers? Thou art
more lovely and less salty though salt of the earth always
references thee. Though
the unacknowledged legislators of the poesy
deny thy beauty you retain irreplaceability.
To a summer's day compare thee
laurelled with thy permanence.
How best to thank thee who pins my sky in place?

THIS PHARMACY, MY GALLERY

Mounted tokens. Bells and razors.

Here, enhance ego, there, suppress
anxiety, weigh the probability
of smudging out cellulite.

Memory lane:
conception was something I would
fend off. Sometimes pay a little extra to be festive,
or fruity, or somehow, furry
handcuffed. Pull out
reading glasses. These
flavoured slicks must be
for a child I did not contracept.
Open one and sip
spermicidal strawberry.

LET FACTS COLLECT

Let them go out of style. Let them be refuted.
Let the facts retreat.

Pin landscape to page. Regret
not being in the more beautiful place. And
time.

Elbows out, hold breath. Only the living
can do this. Look out to the roof.

Count circles. Smell pages.
See if anyone catches me.

Arm under blanket. Shadow on sand. A tree
bears the moon.

There might be a street I haven't walked on yet. Each fact
in the shadow of the previous. Let me

hold faded facts, stand back and watch me
believe.

WHEN I MET JOACHIM

When I met Joachim it was one to one correspondence. He had responded to every one of my letters and we had both memorized all of his screenplays. Our eyes were all four of them brown so there was no problem with that. I had cut my lip rather deeply and we would line up there too.

The strumming of the guitar and some of the accents he could school me on.

He needed a witness and I was just that. I saw it all and I saw Joachim. I walked him; I ran him. I came to weigh the same as him.

We sat back to back. The list of no problems went on and on.

By the end of the first minute I was the same age as him and had the same birthday. Each of our memories matched. The towels appeared with our same names stitched on cotton. Really good cotton.

TOO MUCH ACTIVITY IN EMOTIONAL CENTERS

A numb bum is for the best
there you go take a rest

nurses keep feelings
clipped to their chests

the sound of a banana peeling
nakedness, Unlocked doors

safety first wait while decision
making centres grow.

So poor in language, scramble
to mimic the sound of the brush

when the bowl is not full
and the yellow and green are swirling,

all this resistance, the plunger
pushing and pulling

straining the elbow,
sweat when it first appears

on the clean brow, the ivory soap
resisting the body that wants only

to cool itself. Coffee sucked into dentures
the disappointment of entry points

barriers accepting stains
and aftertaste rearranged

into the roof of the mouth
just as leaky as any bedroom,

this crevice.

EVERYONE'S EXCITED FOR THE PRELUDE TO BE OVER

Getting to the lude. That's where its at. The
pronouns and commas melt
away the dalliance there the room a scene
set and the bed so cushioned the springs in
the spine reminds every rib to keep
the lungs in. Skip the prelude. Don't let its
place at the beginning fool you.

HAIKU FOR THE APPROPRIATION OF CULTURE

A gentleman

Defined himself, commented:
Time to get some Comet
Cum at your side

date night

I got you a skull ring and rohypnol.

what the virgo said

Hello Miss Perfect
What's your lumbar saying
Bend over, give us a gander

prosthetic lilacs

for prosthetic mourners
these dolls will mourn
you
for us.

the birds

stop talking when I
walk under their tree

the lake

said to me
I'm a river
get it right.

this cup

guarantees 15 minutes of pleasure
          who among us can say the same

MAKE A NECKLACE

A trinket. That's right.
A souvenir of what was here

Many bars, coffee shops and bookstores
must be avoided. The day has become

so hopeless that a
novel surfaces

from a handbag. Check
out what made Joyce so damn

important. It's a yearbook of every scholar
who ever wrote about

him. All those faces ink forms.

A TREE CASTS ITS SHADOW ON HIS FACE

A blessing
goes back to bed. Nothing more
will happen. The epilogue
is on its way. Arrange pills
into a sandwich stack. An orange
and white clubhouse. Then the shots
just pour shots
the mouth is glass
enough. Dentures are the stuff
that cups are made of.

THERE ARE A THOUSAND WAYS TO GET OVER YOURSELF

Cosmopolitan lists only 30.
The kitchen can't be red.

That would be far too
obvious. It must be the light.

And that Eiffel Tower. Someone
left it here.

All these shoes heeled
with Eiffel Towers.

Just stay horizontal.
Consciousness cannot be rated.

HOW TO START A FIGHT

Leave a constellation of coffee
grinds on the counter,

wear a scarf that needs to be ironed,
change Gods without signalling,

objectify the incumbent president,
misquote quotable quotes.

Jab pencils around my eye.
Defy gravity. Let it defy me.

THE FINER THINGS FROM THE RIGHT HONORABLE REFINERY FOR THE FINEST REFINED PEOPLE

The water flavoured coffee has hints
of discounted biscuits.

There are yellow squares for afters.

Karen can taste lemon and granules
of sugar. Her mother has one too,

revealing its flavour.

A FINGER'S DISTANCE AWAY

Held feather up in front of the house. Paws gathered unplucked. Karen's purple tank top soda moustache framed Birdie's feather.

Yellow streaks across plate, hardened teabag. Sugar bowl. She packed tobacco into the roller. Whistled air into the paper. Pulled the clasp. Pushed it out popped it off the dispenser. The flyers. Where to buy more milk and eggs. She'll walk to the sweet shop pay the extra just to keep out of a taxi and the velour seats, the seven dollar ride. Who authors the flyers. She never sees the mailman. She don't want to go to Dominions. Kids in carts crying for bars. Someone asked not to eat the bars before they're paid for. The sweet shop is just in and out. The cubes of twenty-five cent Cadbury chocolate. Windowless: hot boxing the sweet smells

PUT KETTLE ON

Degree of burns
Scrape and learn
Courier water
Funnel fantasy
Whip crack mister
Ham down fist her
Chicken rot sifter
Sigh in the butter
Warm thigh blaster
Never enough taster
Slider forty ladies
Feudal fried fillies
Don't call it an emergency

MAKING SMALL TALK IN HEAVEN IS NO EASIER

Turns out

Being dumb is no excuse
Head nods galore

Be still beating heart while pistons pair

pontificate pulse nod pulse toes

Offer

Agreement subtle eyebrow
head tilt and Weather no
beginning proximity to hellfire

brag the distance

a silent secluded circle of hell
good cycling rating

In my hood don't mention the
hood

In my hood store steak

Gullible Gulliver Fulliver and
haggle fist to table The space

he made in her hood worth less
than a dollar

Take my daughter

Please

THE BASEMENT NEEDS FUCKING

Cement is
willing; flesh is weak. Get
Betsy off. Jet spray. Jacks.
Sprain. Burn. Ajax. Separate.

Styrofoam
shrivels. Re-move. Move.
Bag. Bond. Cement. Shell. Wait.
Dream. Wave. Blood. Bar.
Wipe. Frame. Sea breeze.

Cement accepts
water, cement oozes, covers
femur, cement, wet cement
and see what drives form, for
mom, seek, more, knowledge,
knowledgeable to see. Lay in
peace full river bed. Please
you make me see why you
make me sync
you fondly
river bed
heaviest always wins may it
please you
see if you saw
he who is
are you me
see you for long
I see Q see

you longer I saw seeing you
saw

            find the way to
move to fill full. Crush femur in
the Falls Falls Falls Falls

THE HEAD IMPACT BLOND OR BLACK

this punch this judy this email this fifty. this bed floats bedknobs and sticks. sticks and right hook, crochet on the west end.

no damn good and this hood will fit for ever.

make it back this bicycle on the third floor, so cozy with the screen doing what screens do and keep the sun out. this is the dark room.

this corn syrup has the rooster on the side water that down rub the alcohol into the blond or black. black and tan and nothing fermented.

keep it in the ears the concussion will not
be blond or black, something on her arm says will and body

free will goes back to something no cartesian wanted to take credit for.

Just walk him to Siberia simple snow keep it in the pockets this soup for you little memory in the blond.

so short term she speaks all day for the toilet, made new with fair fingers bare bingers. Cupboards full of shaving cream keep it smooth this mattress not called king for a reason. The mechanic at Prud'homme et Sherbrooke will say, Ça va bien.

THE INTERIM LOVERS

Heavy pussied in the willow.
Conniption fit about a $100 piece
of metal a gift unused for 8 years.
The dilettante falls down.

Trumpet her lost afternoons, Narcissus'
swim.   If it is a gift the price should not
be known.   If it is a logical statement

it will balance.   If it cuts it will result
in revenge, revelry and reckoning. Turns
out the r is more than a growl.

The hand Parkinsonian. No commercial will do it
better, the director's name withheld. Anytime
the ingenue holds her breath her cheeks respond

such is bewitching twitching no need for pinching
no slap wasted. Strawberries folded into her silk.
May her diary recount the amount of spoiling that spoiled her hand.

Silver inflames the bull. The china shop of
Place Ville Marie marble wimpers. No comment.
The fine print pores to pour over again with the milk.

Mention prison in passing as if the corpus isn't cell enough.
Resist another panopticon. In passing, Foucault's mother was number
one. The ingenue doesn't wonder what people think

she's on. Disgusting bread has its own restaurant
not even that bad in purgatory.
These cars exoskeletal.

Horoscope says avoid ex lovers.

GRENADA

nother hanging fanged

The frown frontal fade
flow feather
forge flummoxed floundering follicles
found fowl fair fondle fondly
fog fade flow feather fade fix
fend fentanyl fight
fade flippers fracking

franchise five foil frame father
four flushed fated floor feathers fussed fairs fairies fed fists
forced flight. phone fibbed
forehead fobbed fibrilated fibre knobbed fishbones

Foire fastronomique armoire fraîche.
Farewell Fair well. well. be that.

NOTE LIZARD'S SILENCE

The convenience of his diet.

W.W. deuce.   Bee stung tongue.   Bespoke bikes.

No single religion's customs to adopt

Tracing has always been painful
With the fingers flattened
The nose plugged.

DAY BOX BEES

week endlong buzzing. and dared to. carryboxhome.
again regululation. the stings the approach the box
the bell the boost the box seed.

wanted two lookfeel

ugly each body so much ugliness the stalls white
making danger much. should be red. read the ship
ping and handling
again. queen be checked on. fearn't payment,
lockdoor. fortyeight hours' air.

Caution from Algonquin.

she neverminded broken vases, comical, 400 dollar vase more fool eye of the need ill. bit of hanpain't on a ting. golden gloved hand? cash and meer onto a prosthetic pussycat. none of these made sense, some bees already dead, these fallen, bodies must be hollow, own lee t'wood makeup the mass. hoe acorn four. no body anne sirred foam. fitness package. may be maid addin'. great. shore-broken tube tragic, such thick glass threw glue, cracker

news. find the queen, beginnerstips on how to, want to find queen. 70 years sold sent bax. dynamite sticks marred up on the side. a puff of smoke, get 'em runnin 'round, top off, easy does it.

tampered box would be. talk of vine the pohst ahffice, switch tape sleeve itt oot for ein mint. a'nother. just forgetted too tape. dry goods the saddle'sbags. lastend soap-box.

a solid honey. very the queen thee.

one thing with us.

family-ize, square bodies. on the tail. no stinger, how to study the reasoning being they will wise her to the lowcare queen. th'eyes drone rollbody. the drone looks wise.

raise it up. solo her hand lost all previous muscle memory.

the drone not short short. mercy. brutalin' honey frame. queen's farside too, dayseekinglight

Doreen sets in the window.

all queens are not alike, a small bite on the hand. a solid brood, a little honey at the top lip.

don't spend a whole lot of time on each side, a fraction
of the weekend. see eggs
on the side, the queen has been
on this side within recent pasts.

anticipate the queen.

thee queen has a lot of yellow, she’s not
a runner, she’s not
a hider.

APPENDIX

Keep eyes on the road an's upon wheel

or tear the trees, know they are prettier
than poetry.

May your punctuation always be punitive.

ACKNOWLEDGEMENTS

Thank you Mom, Joelle, Rob, Maggie, Kathleen, Eva, Angela, Natalie, Katie, Michael, Anh, Janette, Melissa, Penny and Paul. Thanks Jim, for doing this book with me.

Thank you to the Ontario Arts Council for funding through the Writers' Reserve Program.

Thank you to the editors of the following journals:

Rusty Toque #6: "Mapplethorpe's Bourgeois"

The Writing Disorder Winter 2013-14: "Behold"; "Raining Coins"

The Puritan #27: "Portrait Of Isabel Rawsthorne Standing In A Street In Soho, 1967"; "My Life It Stood A Market Ready Product"

CV2, Spring 2015: "Machines at Rust";"Struggle Within"

Riddle Fence #25: "Note the Lizard's Silence"; "When I met"

ABOUT THE AUTHOR

Angela Hibbs' previous books are *Sin Eater* (Arbeiter Ring 2015), *Wanton* (Insomniac Press, 2009) and *Passport* (DC Books, 2006).